WHAT ARE YOU SLEEPING WITH?

Sunday Bradley

BK
ROYSTON
Publishing

BK Royston Publishing
P. O. Box 4321
Jeffersonville, IN 47131
502-802-5385
http://www.bkroystonpublishing.com
bkroystonpublishing@gmail.com

© Copyright – 2018

Cover Design: Brent Barnett by
besquaredgraphicdesign@gmail.com

ISBN: 978-1-946111-62-3

Printed in the United States of America

DEDICATION

I would like to dedicate this book to all the women, young ladies and teenage girls around the world. My prayer is that there is awakening in your spirit so you don't have to sleep with any issue and can move forward in the plan and purpose in life that God has for you.

ACKNOWLEDGMENTS

I would first like to thank God for being in every part of my life I couldn't have done this out with God, "The lord Jesus Christ" my savior. To my mother, Rosella Brown, for her encouraging words while writing this book thanks "Rosie." To the man I call daddy, Dennis Winburn, I thank you for stepping in, when you didn't have to and you did.

A special acknowledgment to my husband, Maurice Bradley for pushing me when I don't feel like it and keeping me grounded in the word of God. I will love you always... hubby.

Two my Daughters, Brittany Foree and Jasmine Foree, my love is never ending. You're the best parts of me. I will forever be grateful for the best gift you could have given me, my grandchildren, Lilly, Xavier and Toussaint. To Jemaine Russell Jr, "Maine" I love you to the moon and back. To the Traveling Squad, Bonita Owens, Stephine Owens, Shaunda Owens, may God continually let us travel from city to city and from country to country making memories and laughter until we become the "Golden Girls." To everyone in the Winburn, Owens, Bradley and Foree family, I love you.

Finally, a very special acknowledgement to Portland Memorial Missionary Baptist Church.

TABLE OF CONTENTS

INTRODUCTION

This book is not to condemn you but to help you recognize what you are sleeping with. Have you ever heard the old saying, "If you lay down with a dog, you're going to get up with fleas?" Likewise, if you go to bed every night with the same issue or issues, you will get up with them every morning. Let's put these issues to rest forever.

The first step to doing this is to understand the power of your tongue. You can't do anything without first saying you're going to overcome any issue that you're sleeping with. Second, get with someone you trust who you can tell anything to and they won't judge you. Don't ask that bitter, hater, or undercover backstabber so-called friend because you know who she or he is in the group. Third, write-down what you think your issue is and then compare your notes to your friend's. Now if you feel you don't have any issue or issues, put this book down. "We all have sinned and fallen short of the glory of God." So, when you are ready to stand in your truth for what it is, you can start to change with God's help. God wants us to be free from all the things holding us back from being what He has called us to be. I pray that this book gives you information, revelation or confirmation.

"Wash me inside and out from my wrongdoing and make me clean from my sin"

Psalm 51:2 (NLV)

Chapter One
Self

No one has your DNA or finger prints in the world. God made you to be you. Everything starts with you and how you handle a situation. Were you too emotional when you made a major decision? Or are you doing the best you can or you just easing by? Did you pray before making a major decision? There is always time to make changes in your life to better yourself. However, there comes a time in everyone's life when we should know who we are, even if it's good, bad or ugly.

Then Jesus said to them all, "If anyone wants to follow Me, he must give up himself and his own desires. He must take up his cross every day and follow Me."

Luke 9:23 NLV

What's Under Your Covers?

You must ask yourself, and be honest, "What am I sleeping with?" Here are a few examples and if something is not on this list, please add it on the next page.

Jealousy	Selfish
Strife	Rebellion
Envy	Mismanaging of money
Pride	Drugs
Manipulator	Adultery
Gossiper	Liar
Bitterness	
Backstabber	
Deceiver	
Slothfulness	
Procrastination	
Fornication	

What am I sleeping with? (What you think or know?)

_____

_____

_____

_____

_____

_____

What someone you trust said….

_____

_____

_____

_____

_____

_____

_____

3

What's On Your Back?

When there are strongholds in your life, it can hold you back from moving forward. Strong holds can be anything that is not of God, such as lying, cheating, fornication, stealing also manipulating and being deceitful. Gambling, alcohol and drugs are like spending money you know you don't have. First, ask yourself why you do it? If you said, "Because I can," that is the answer a child would say. Maybe there was something in your childhood or your past that triggered a stronghold. When you have a stronghold, it's just the cover of the real problem underneath. You must remember God didn't design us to have strongholds. If there is a stronghold, constantly pray and have others praying on your behalf. There are parts to remember when letting go of a stronghold and they each start with the letter 'R.'

- Realizing and understanding the strong hold

- Remove yourself from the situation

- Repent of your sin

- Receive the word of God

"For the weapons of our warfare not carnal, but mighty

through God to the pulling down of strong holds."

2 Corinthians 10:4 (KJV)

Speak It

Some people have died by the words they have said, for example, 'I can't make it' or 'I can't do it.' If you say these things, it will come to pass. Or, if you're on a diet and you're continually saying I can't lose any weight, then you won't. Or, 'I'm broke' 'I don't have any money,' then you will be broke. Have you heard somebody say, 'It's always something.' Don't agree with them because you are speaking that there will always be something wrong going on in your life also. And the worst of them all is, if you tell your child or another family member, 'You are no good just like your daddy.' You are speaking over that child's future without even knowing it. Stop saying bad things about your life and the lives of others. Your words have lots of power, so choose your words carefully.

"Death and life are in the power of the tongue."

Proverbs 18:21 (KJV)

Change Your Stinking Thinking

Don't be a 'negative Naida.' Start your day with positive thinking, like, 'Today is going to be a great day,' or 'I feel good today and I look good too.' Renew your mind to 'positive Patty.' Instead of thinking I can't do this, think I'm going to get through this. Or, 'What I'm going through now is only for a moment, this will not break me but it will develop me.' You must renew your mind. Also, stop being negative when other people have good news to tell, because when you say something negative, people hear it and see it.

"And do not be conformed to this world, but be transformed by the renewing of your mind."

Romans 12:2 (NKJV)

Mind Your Own Business

If you're taking care of your own business, then you don't have time to be in somebody else's business. When you mind your own business, life is less stressful. Life is more peaceful. Most of the time when people are always in somebody else's business, they don't want to deal with their own life nor do they have anything going on in their life.

Make it your ambition to lead a quiet life to mind your own business and to work with your hands.

1 Thessalonians 4:11 ESV

What You Put In Will Come Out

Respect your body, as you would want somebody else to. Why are you disrespecting your body? Don't eat everything you see because you can. Not everybody is the same size, but you can still be healthy. Drugs and alcohol are only a temporary fix and they both do more damage to your body in the long run. Using them could cause a lifetime of body pain. Put the junk down, start getting more rest, eat right and exercise. Find a day of the week and do something that you like that's not toxic to your body. You only have one body so take care it.

"Do you not know that your bodies are temples of the Holy Spirit?"

1 Corinthians 6:19 (NIV)

Take a Hold

It's okay to have emotions. Take control of your emotions. Don't make decisions when you're upset or grieving. If you are emotional about a situation, you will probably make the wrong decision. Instead, stop and take control of your emotions. If something takes you out of who you normally are, then step back and examine your emotions. Don't let anyone change your character.

"Fools give full vent to their rage, but the wise bring calm in the end."

Proverbs 29: 11 (NIV)

The Cover Up

When you tell a lie, people know when you're lying. Telling lies hurts everybody involved. If you tell a lie, you always must remember what you said, but the truth doesn't change. A lie is like weeds in a yard, it always comes back up. And there is no truth in a lie, people don't respect a liar.

"The Lord detests lying lips, but he delights in people who are trustworthy."

Proverbs 12:22 (NIV)

Talking Time

Pray as many times a day as you can. Put it in your schedule, when you wake up in the morning. Pray in the bathroom, at the kitchen table, in your car or on the bus. Pray on your breaks at work or school. Pray before you go to bed. Prayer can change things. The more you pray, the more you stay connected with God. God is the best listener. God answers prayers the same way he did years and years ago.

"Rejoice always; pray continually, give thanks in all circumstances; for this is God's will for you in Christ Jesus."

1 Thessalonians 5:16-18 (NIV)

A Helping Hand

Make time to help someone at your local shelter. Maybe you can serve food or help clean up. Help those in need at a nursing home. Join a committee at your local church that will fit your personality. Volunteering does the soul good. Always help those who are in need.

"Whatever you do, work at it with all your heart, as working for the Lord, not for the human masters."

Colossians 3:23 (NIV)

Self…

_____

_____

_____

_____

_____

_____

_____

_____

_____

_____

_____

_____

_____

_____

_____

_____

_____

_____

Self…

Self…

_____

_____

_____

_____

_____

_____

_____

_____

_____

_____

_____

_____

_____

_____

_____

Chapter Two
Relationships

Relationships are a state of involving mutual dealings between people.

If you are single, this is the time for you to work on you. If there is something you need in your life to be better, then go for it. This is the time to get mentally, physically and spiritually stronger. Why would you want to go into a relationship unprepared? Maybe that's why it didn't work out last time. If you are beginning with the best you can be, then you'll get the best in return because you won't settle for less. Get your house in order. Get that degree you always wanted. Get into an exercise class. Do you first! It's better to be happy by yourself, than miserable with someone else.

If you are married, always communicate with your spouse about what you need from one another. Don't stop growing. Grow together and pray together. Try new things to keep the marriage exciting. Remember in a marriage there will be good days and there may be bad days, but you vowed for better or for worse to take the road of life together.

"There is a time for everything, and a season for every activity under heavens."

Ecclesiastes 3:1 (NIV)

Would You Date Yourself?

Are you rude, resentful, selfish, maybe bitter, controlling, or unwilling to trust because the last relationship has left you this way? Do you always have to win every argument or always have to be right? Don't date anybody until you are dateable. Don't start dating when you are emotionally down or broken from the last relationship. If you do, you will put up with the wrong thing. Would you date someone with the same issues that you have under your covers? Take some time to examine yourself. Take the time off from dating and be celibate while you understand who you are and what you want.

If you are dating, you might want to ask yourself if he's a 15 or 20-minute man, or a 15 or 20-year man? If he can't pray with you, why let him lay with you? Will he still date you if you tell him you're celibate? A man who knows and loves the Lord should respect you and your wishes.

"Love is patient and kind; love does not envy or boast; it is not arrogant or rude. It does not insist on its own way; it is not irritable or resentful; it does not rejoice at wrongdoing, but rejoices with the truth. Love bears all things, believes all things, hopes all things, endures all things."

1 Corinthians 13:4-7 (ESV)

Who Said It?

If you know someone who is always talking about somebody else (the Gossiper), then more than likely she is talking about you too. You really don't need that negativity in your life. Just politely say to the Gossiper the next time he/she calls, "I'm sorry, but I don't want to hear it because it doesn't have anything to do with me." If you listen, you're sitting in on judgment. And if it does have something to do with you, don't listen to the middleman always get it straight from the source.

Brothers and sisters, do not slander one another. Anyone who speaks against a brother or sister or judges them speaks against the law and judges it. When you judge the law, you are not keeping it, but sitting in judgment on it.

James 4:11 (NIV)

The Company You Keep

When you are hanging around bad company, people will think you're doing the same thing even if you're not. While hanging with bad company, there are things that can happen to change your life and not for the good. These things could stop you from moving up to your next level. When you're with bad company, there is no need to be rude to them. Just step back and give them space and pray that God shows them the error of their ways. Ask God for wisdom so you're not lead around by bad company.

"Do not be misled, bad company corrupts good character."

1 Corinthians 15:33 (NIV)

Keep It Moving

You must forgive those who hurt you. What happened in the past is over. Don't carry unforgiveness and anger in your heart. That was the past and the definitions of past means: no longer current, gone by: it's over. Whoever has hurt you has moved on with their life and your holding on to unforgiveness. Don't let anyone take your joy because they won't give it back. Don't give them anything but forgiveness. Don't give them anymore power. Drop it and keep it moving. If someone has hurt you, it will come back around to them whether you believe in karma or reaping what is sowed. If you forgive them, God will forgive you of your sins because we all have sinned.

"Never take your own revenge, beloved, but leave room for the wrath of God, for it is written, "Vengeance Is Mine, I Will Repay," says the Lord

Romans 12:19 (NASB)

Fornication

Fornication is seriously dangerous, even when you are trying to be safe. One small mistake and you can contract something that you may have to deal with for the rest of your life or it could take your life. Save yourself for the right man. He will respect you more, if you're not giving it up to every man you meet. If you are fornicating, you are the one getting used in the end. A man will go on about his life and would not think twice about you because men are physical. They are not fascinated easily because fornication is physical. Women who fornicate with a lot of different men have some underlining issues and it's really not about going to bed for them. She may have been molested, looking for the father figure she never had, or she is trying to find love because no man has ever shown her love. She may not feel pretty or attractive and thinks that's the only she can and will get her love. But, you must remember, God made you beautiful. A man should never define you by taking you to bed with him.

There is much more to you than going to bed with you.

"Flee fornication. Every sin that a man doeth is without the

body; but he that committeth fornication sinneth against his

own body."

1 Corinthians 6:18 (KJV)

The Wifey Type

Now if you're looking for a husband, you're wrong. The Bible scripture says, 'He who finds a wife, finds a good thing.' It doesn't say anywhere in the Bible, 'She who finds a husband...' So are you conducting and preparing yourself to be a wife? You can't do single things if your wanting to be a wife. Are you out there acting like popcorn, popping yourself from man to man? Popcorn popping means: I went to dinner with Billy on Monday, then on Friday, Mark took me for drinks, and Saturday night you got with your male friend with benefits. A man looks at that without letting you know. A man doesn't want a woman if she doesn't have herself together or is getting herself together. A man doesn't want a woman who will bring him down, because every morning he leaves his home he has to deal with the drama of the outside world. He wants something real to come home to because her beauty and big butt will only last for so long. What do you have that you can bring to the table? Can you cook a meal or clean house? Will you hold him up if he falls?

Can you budget money or are you willing to compromise for

the greater good of someone else?

"He who finds a wife finds a good thing."

Proverbs 18:22 (NKJV)

Number 2

If you're the side chick, mistress, or the other woman and think no one knows what you're doing, you're wrong. Why do you think it's going to turn out right when it started wrong? Don't believe he is going to make you the main one or even wifey, because he thinks your standards are low, and because you know he has someone else and you're dealing with it. You are basically his slave and it is all about when he can get with you. Then when you do, it's all about what he wants to do. He is wasting your time. You're not his woman because he has a main chick at home. They are living their life together, and you're the one waiting around for the phone call or a text and life is moving forward. Yes, he may be paying you, but is it really worth it in the end?

With the Number 2 Law Book You Get

- No rights. If he can't make it at the last minute, you can't complain about anything.

- No holidays. He will be with his family you might get a 3 or 4-minute phone call.

- No real comfort. He can't be there full time when you're just having a bad day, sick or just need someone to hold you.

- No real benefits. He is not leaving his life insurance to you or his 401k plan if something happens to him because you are 'Number 2.' Two never wins the race only number one.

You are worth more than that. You're a queen and should be treated as one. He is not going to leave her, no matter how miserable he says he is. Furthermore, if he does leave her, can you ever trust him? Remember how you got him is how you will lose him.

"There is nothing concealed that will not be disclosed, or hidden that will not be made known."

Luke 12:2 (NIV)

Relationships...

_____

_____

_____

_____

_____

_____

_____

_____

_____

_____

_____

_____

_____

_____

_____

Relationships...

Chapter 3

Money

We sometimes get emotional about our money because we worked hard for it. However, remember God was the one who blessed you with it. If you take care of God's business, He will take care of yours. Money can be here today and gone tomorrow. But God is everlasting.

"No one can serve two masters. Either you will hate the one and love the other, or you will be devoted to the one and despise the other. You cannot serve both God and money."

Matthew 6:24 (NIV)

Ten Percent

Tithing is giving ten percent of your earnings to your church. There are people with many different views on this, but I'm a believer in tithing. When you make 100% and you give only 10%, I believe the tithing covers the 90% to produce more. Would you rather have a blessed 90% rather than a cursed 100%?

"Bring all the tithes into the storehouse, That there may be food in my house, And try me now in this, Says the Lord of hosts."

Malachi 3:10 (NKJV)

Get Up and Get Out

You must get up and go get it. It may not come knocking on your front door and if it does, you still have to work to maintain it. If you have an idea or some type of dream for a small business, going back school, getting a job or better job, then go for it. Get up, get out, and go and get it. The best thing is to do, and the worse thing is not to do.

"Lazy hands make for poverty, but diligent hands bring wealth."

Proverbs 10:4 (NIV)

The Give ME's

You should always want to help somebody but use your common sense. Don't be a fool. There are some people who you can give and give to and they are never satisfied. They are called the 'Give ME's.' 'Can you give me some money?' (And they don't pay it back). They sit around and wait for your payday at work and the first thing they say is, "I know you got paid today, can you just give me something." Helping people is a blessing, but don't be an enabler. Some people will take your kindness as weakness.

"Do not give dogs what is scared; do not throw your pearls to pigs. If you do, they may trample then under their feet, and turn and tear you to pieces."

Matthew 7:6 (NIV)

Out of Control

Overspending seems harmless at first.   However, when you get use to spending more than you have, it becomes a big problem and that is spending money that you don't even have yet. Paying bills is like a cat and mouse game. Overspending brings four underlining issues besides overspending.

- Overwhelmed

- Stress

- Can't sleep at night

- Depression

Furthermore, we might do things for money that we thought we would never do to just get out of debt. Get with a financial adviser before things get out of hand.

"The plans of the diligent lead surely to abundance, but everyone who is hasty comes only to poverty."

Proverbs 21:5 (ESV)

Money...

_____

_____

_____

_____

_____

_____

_____

_____

_____

_____

_____

_____

_____

_____

_____

Money...

_____

_____

_____

_____

_____

_____

_____

_____

_____

_____

_____

_____

_____

Chapter 4
The Four Center Cores of
Bad Behavior

Jealously

Don't be jealous of your neighbor, because you don't know what it took for them to get what they have. You could be looking at the end result. There could have been months and years of planning, struggle, tears, heartbreak even disappointment. So, if jealously is there, ask yourself: Could I take what they took? In the whole process not just the end of it.

"Sure resentment destroys the fool, and jealousy kills the simple."

Job 5:2 (NLT)

Pride

Don't be ashamed to ask for help, pride comes before the fall of destruction. Sometimes it is what it is. Don't be filled with pride, you should be humble. Pride will make you think you did it all on your own. You're not an island to yourself God brings people in your life for reasons and resources.

"Haughty eyes, a proud heart, and evil actions are all sin."

Proverb 21:4 (NLT)

Strife

Be careful of what you say. Don't hold on to strife because it will turn to resentment and hate. Don't be disrespectful when you speak, instead say it in love. It's not what you say; it's how you say it. Don't go to bed with strife, because when you wake up the next day it's stronger and you have to deal with the problem head on. Strife is a chameleon and it will change into other things.

Keep away from strife is an honor for a man, but any fool will quarrel.

Proverbs 20:3 (NASB)

Envy

Never compare yourself to others. What is for you is for you. God has a plan and a purpose just for you. Don't be envious because you have not arrived where you want to be yet and someone else has. You will get there. There is a season for everybody, but you must be ready when it comes.

Let not your heart envy sinners, but continue in the fear of the Lord all the day.

Proverbs 23:17 (ESV)

Bad Behavior...

_____

_____

_____

_____

_____

_____

_____

_____

_____

_____

_____

_____

_____

Bad Behavior...

_____

_____

_____

_____

_____

_____

_____

_____

_____

_____

_____

_____

_____

Seven Things God Hates

A proud look

A lying tongue

Hands that shed innocent blood

A heart that deviseth wicked imaginations

Feet that be swift in running to mischief

A false witness that speaketh lies

He that soweth discord among brethren

Proverbs 6:16-19 (KJV)

I Am A Virtuous Woman

I am a virtuous woman because I will teach my children the ways of the Lord, and to love nothing more than Him.

I am a virtuous woman because I know beauty is skin deep.

I am a virtuous woman because I can work hard with my hands as well as my mind.

I am a virtuous woman because I can make my house a home no matter how big or small it may be.

I am a virtuous woman because I can help others and expect nothing in return.

I am a virtuous woman because I know my time is precious and I won't waste it on foolishness.

I am a virtuous woman because if I may fall, I will get up stronger the next time.

I am a virtuous woman, single with a strong mind, body and spirit.

I am a virtuous woman because I respect my husband, pray with my husband, and I will submit to my husband.

I am a virtuous woman because I love the Lord with all my heart and all that I am.

I am a virtuous woman because I know the Lord loves me because of who I am.

Based on Proverbs 31

I can do all things through Christ which strengtheneth me.

Philippians 4:13 (KJV)

www.ingramcontent.com/pod-product-compliance
Lightning Source LLC
Chambersburg PA
CBHW071949100426
42736CB00042B/2645